DACHSHUND SURVIVAL GUIDE

How to Train Your Dachshund

Dale C. Randall

Table of Contents

INTRODUCTION

Welcome to "Dachshund Survival Guide: How to Train Your Dachshund." This guide is your comprehensive resource for understanding and training your Dachshund, a breed known for its unique personality and distinct characteristics. Whether you're a first-time pet owner or an experienced dog enthusiast, this book offers specific, actionable advice tailored to the needs of Dachshunds.

Dachshunds, often affectionately called wiener dogs or sausage dogs, are small but mighty canines with a spirited character. Training them requires a blend of patience, consistency, and an understanding of their unique traits. This guide is crafted to help you navigate through the joys and challenges of training your Dachshund, covering everything from basic obedience and housebreaking to addressing breed-specific behavior issues.

We delve into practical training techniques and step-by-step instructions that are specifically suited to the Dachshund's temperament and physical capabilities. Learn how to effectively communicate with your Dachshund, utilize positive reinforcement, and build a strong bond based on mutual trust and respect. From tackling common behavioral problems like excessive barking and digging to introducing advanced training concepts, this guide provides detailed strategies to help you and your Dachshund succeed.

Embrace the journey of training your Dachshund with this specialized guide. Let's begin this adventure together, and discover the full potential of your beloved companion.

CHAPTER 1: UNDERSTANDING DACHSHUNDS

This chapter provides essential insights into the unique nature and needs of Dachshunds, setting a strong foundation for effective training. Known for their distinctive appearance and spirited character, Dachshunds require a training approach that addresses their specific traits. Here, we'll explore their history, personality, and behavioral tendencies, equipping you with the knowledge to tailor your training methods effectively. This chapter is your first step towards fostering a harmonious and rewarding relationship with your pet.

The History and Background of Dachshunds

Dachshunds, with their distinctive elongated bodies and short legs, are one of the most recognizable dog breeds in the world. But do you know the fascinating history behind these adorable little dogs? In this subchapter, we will explore the origins and background of Dachshunds, shedding light on their unique characteristics and why they make such wonderful pets.

Originally bred in Germany during the 15th century, Dachshunds were primarily used for hunting small game, particularly badgers, hence their name which translates to "badger dog" in German. Their long and narrow body, combined with their exceptional sense of smell, made them perfect for digging into burrows and flushing out prey. Over time, Dachshunds also became adept at hunting other animals like rabbits and foxes.

The breed's distinctive appearance can be attributed to their specific hunting purpose. Their elongated bodies helped them maneuver through narrow tunnels, while their short legs allowed them to dig efficiently. Dachshunds also possess a strong jaw and sharp teeth, which were essential for their hunting duties.

During the 19th century, Dachshunds gained popularity not only as hunting companions but also as beloved family pets. Their friendly, intelligent, and loyal nature made them endearing to pet owners of all kinds. Queen Victoria, a well-known dog lover, played a significant role in popularizing the breed in England.

As Dachshunds became more popular, different varieties emerged. Today, there are three main coat types: smooth-haired, wire-haired, and long-haired Dachshunds. Each type has its own unique set of characteristics and grooming needs.

While their hunting instincts have diminished over time, Dachshunds still retain their determination and feisty nature. This can sometimes present challenges when it comes to training. However, with the right techniques and patience, Dachshunds can be trained to become well-behaved and obedient pets.

Different Types and Varieties of Dachshunds

When it comes to Dachshunds, there are several different types and varieties that pet owners should be aware of. These unique characteristics not only make them visually appealing but also play a role in their temperament and physical abilities. In this subchapter, we will explore the various types and varieties of Dachshunds, providing valuable insights for pet owners interested in training these lovable canines.

Firstly, let's discuss the three main types of Dachshunds based on their coat texture: smooth-haired, wire-haired, and long-haired. Smooth-haired Dachshunds have short, sleek coats that require minimal grooming. Wire-haired Dachshunds, on the other hand, possess a coarse, thick outer coat with a dense undercoat, making them more suitable for colder climates. Lastly, long-haired Dachshunds have silky, flowing coats that require regular brushing to prevent matting.

Additionally, Dachshunds come in two sizes: standard and miniature. Standard Dachshunds typically weigh between 16-32 pounds and stand around 8-9 inches tall. Miniature Dachshunds, as the name suggests, are smaller, weighing between 11-16 pounds and standing about 5-6 inches tall. It is important to consider the size when training a Dachshund, as their exercise needs may differ.

Furthermore, Dachshunds can be classified into three different coat patterns: solid, dapple, and piebald. Solid Dachshunds have a uniform coat color without any markings. Dapple Dachshunds have a mottled pattern with lighter spots on a darker base coat. Lastly, piebald Dachshunds have large patches of white on their coat, often combined with another color.

Each type and variety of Dachshund may exhibit varying temperaments and tendencies. For example, smooth-haired Dachshunds are known for being outgoing and confident, while wire-haired Dachshunds tend to be more stubborn and independent. Long-haired Dachshunds are often described as affectionate and gentle.

Understanding these differences in types and varieties of Dachshunds is essential for pet owners looking to train their furry companions effectively. By recognizing the unique traits associated with each type, owners can tailor their training methods to suit their Dachshund's specific needs. Whether you have a standard smooth-haired Dachshund or a miniature wire-haired Dachshund, being knowledgeable about their individual characteristics will contribute to a successful training journey.

Dachshund Temperament and Characteristics

Understanding the temperament and characteristics of your Dachshund is crucial when it comes to training and raising a well-behaved and happy pet. These delightful little dogs have a unique personality that sets them apart from other breeds. In this subchapter, we will delve into the various aspects of the Dachshund temperament and highlight their distinctive characteristics.

One of the most prominent traits of Dachshunds is their bold and confident nature. Originally bred as hunting dogs, they possess an inherent fearlessness that can sometimes border on stubbornness. This characteristic can make training a Dachshund a challenge, but with patience and consistency, you can channel their determination into positive behaviors.

Dachshunds are known for their loyalty and strong bond with their owners. They form deep attachments and thrive on love and attention. This makes them excellent family pets and companions, as they are always eager to be by your side. However, their loyalty can sometimes lead to separation anxiety, so it is important to gradually introduce them to being alone and provide them with activities to keep them occupied.

Their small size and distinctive elongated bodies make Dachshunds prone to certain health issues, such as back problems and obesity. It is crucial to provide them with a balanced diet and regular exercise to maintain their overall health and prevent weight gain. Additionally, training Dachshunds to use stairs and avoiding activities that put strain on their backs can help minimize the risk of spinal injuries.

Dachshunds are also known for their playful and energetic nature. They love to chase balls, play with toys, and explore their surroundings. Regular exercise and mental stimulation are essential to keep them happy and prevent destructive behaviors that may arise from boredom.

When it comes to training, Dachshunds respond best to positive reinforcement techniques. They thrive on praise and rewards, such as treats and affection. Harsh or forceful training methods can cause them to become stubborn or anxious. Consistency, patience, and using a firm yet gentle approach will yield the best results.

In conclusion, understanding the temperament and characteristics of Dachshunds is vital for successful training and a harmonious relationship with these adorable pets. Their boldness, loyalty, and playful nature make them a joy to be around. By providing them with the right care, exercise, and training, you can ensure that your Dachshund will grow into a well-behaved and happy member of your family.

Common Health Issues in Dachshunds

As pet owners, it is essential to be aware of the common health issues that can affect our beloved Dachshunds. While these adorable sausage-shaped dogs bring joy and companionship into our lives, they are also prone to certain health conditions that require our attention and care. In this subchapter, we will explore the most prevalent health issues in Dachshunds and provide you with valuable insights to ensure your furry friend's well-being.

One of the most common health problems in Dachshunds is Intervertebral Disc Disease (IVDD). Due to their elongated spinal structure, Dachshunds are at a higher risk of developing this condition, which can cause back pain, paralysis, and even loss of bladder control. It is crucial to monitor your Dachshund's activity levels, avoid jumping from heights, and provide them with proper support while climbing stairs or getting on furniture.

Obesity is another prevalent health concern in Dachshunds. Their small size and love for food can easily lead to weight gain, which puts unnecessary strain on their back and joints. Regular exercise, a balanced diet, and portion control are vital to maintain a healthy weight for your Dachshund.

Dachshunds are also prone to dental problems such as gum disease and tooth decay. Their small mouths and crowded teeth make them more susceptible to plaque buildup. Regular dental care, including brushing their teeth and providing appropriate chew toys, can help prevent these issues and ensure good oral hygiene.

Another health issue commonly seen in Dachshunds is allergies. They can be allergic to certain foods, environmental factors like pollen or dust mites, or even flea bites. Watch out for signs of itching, redness, or gastrointestinal issues and consult your veterinarian for proper diagnosis and treatment.

Lastly, Dachshunds are predisposed to eye problems, including cataracts and progressive retinal atrophy (PRA). Regular eye check-ups and early detection are crucial to manage these conditions effectively.

As pet owners, it is our responsibility to be proactive in preventing and managing these health issues. Regular visits to the veterinarian, a well-balanced diet, exercise, and ensuring a safe environment for our Dachshunds are essential for their overall well-being. By staying informed and providing the right care, we can ensure our Dachshunds lead long, healthy, and happy lives.

Remember, our furry friends rely on us for their health, so let's make sure we are well-informed and equipped to provide them with the best care possible.

CHAPTER 2: PREPARING FOR DACHSHUND TRAINING

In this chapter, we dive into the preliminary steps necessary for successful Dachshund training. Preparing for the training journey is as crucial as the training itself. We'll focus on establishing a conducive environment for learning, selecting the right tools and equipment, and creating a structured routine that suits the unique temperament of your Dachshund. Understanding the principle of positive reinforcement, we'll outline how to utilize it effectively to encourage good behavior. This chapter sets the stage, ensuring you and your Dachshund are well-equipped and ready to embark on a rewarding training experience together.

Creating a Safe and Comfortable Environment

When it comes to training your Dachshund, creating a safe and comfortable environment is crucial. A well-designed and secure space will not only promote positive behaviors but also ensure the safety and well-being of your furry friend. In this subchapter, we will explore the essential aspects of creating such an environment.

First and foremost, it is important to establish a designated area for your Dachshund. This can be a specific room or a corner in your home where your pet can feel secure and relaxed. Make sure this space is free from any potential hazards such as electrical cords, toxic plants, or small objects that your Dachshund could swallow. Keep in mind that Dachshunds are known for their curious nature, so a thorough inspection of the area is essential.

Additionally, consider providing your Dachshund with a comfortable bed or crate. Dogs, including Dachshunds, naturally seek out cozy and safe spaces to rest. A well-padded bed or crate will become their sanctuary, a place where they can retreat to relax and feel secure. Introduce the bed or crate early on during the training process to associate it with positive experiences.

Maintaining cleanliness and hygiene is another important aspect of creating a safe and comfortable environment. Regularly clean your Dachshund's living area, including their bed, toys, and any other items they frequently come into contact with. This will help prevent the buildup of dirt, bacteria, and unpleasant odors.

In addition to the physical environment, it is crucial to create a safe and comfortable atmosphere for your Dachshund. This involves providing a consistent routine, clear communication, and positive reinforcement. Dogs thrive on structure and predictable schedules, so establish regular feeding, exercise, and training times. Communicate clearly and effectively using simple commands and positive body language, and always reward your Dachshund for desired behaviors. This will help them feel secure and build trust with you as their owner.

Remember, creating a safe and comfortable environment is an ongoing process. Regularly assess and adjust your

Dachshund's surroundings to ensure they remain safe and conducive to their well-being. By providing a secure and comfortable environment, you are setting the foundation for successful training and a happy and healthy life together with your beloved Dachshund.

Selecting the Right Training Tools and Equipment

As a pet owner, one of the key aspects of training your Dachshund is having the right tools and equipment at your disposal. The right tools can make a significant difference in the effectiveness and efficiency of your training sessions. In this subchapter, we will discuss the essential training tools and equipment that every Dachshund owner should consider.

1. Collars and Harnesses: Collars and harnesses are essential for controlling and restraining your Dachshund during walks and training sessions. For Dachshunds, it is recommended to use a harness instead of a collar to prevent strain on their delicate necks. Look for a well-fitting, comfortable, and adjustable harness that provides proper support.

2. Leashes: A high-quality leash is a must-have for any pet owner. Choose a leash that is sturdy, comfortable to hold, and has a length suitable for your training needs. Retractable leashes are not recommended for training purposes, as they can lead to loss of control and accidents.

3. Clicker: A clicker is a small handheld device that produces a distinct clicking sound. It is used as a marker during training to signal to your Dachshund that they have performed the desired behavior correctly. Clickers are highly effective and can speed up the learning process significantly.

4. Treats: Positive reinforcement is a powerful tool in training any dog, including Dachshunds. Treats are an excellent motivator and reward for good behavior. Select small, soft, and tasty treats that your Dachshund loves. Ensure that the treats are healthy and low in calories to avoid weight gain.

5. Toys: Interactive toys can be a valuable tool in training your Dachshund. Toys that require problem-solving or provide mental stimulation can help keep your Dachshund engaged and focused during training sessions.

6. Training Pads: Training pads can be useful during the housebreaking process. They provide a designated area for your Dachshund to relieve themselves and can help prevent accidents inside the house.

When selecting training tools and equipment, always prioritize your Dachshund's safety and comfort. Avoid tools that cause discomfort or fear, as it can lead to negative associations with training. Additionally, consult with a professional dog trainer or veterinarian for guidance on specific tools or equipment that may be beneficial for your Dachshund's training needs.

Remember, the right tools and equipment are just one aspect of successful Dachshund training. Consistency, patience, and positive reinforcement are equally important in shaping your Dachshund into a well-behaved and happy companion.

Establishing a Routine and Schedule

When it comes to training a Dachshund, establishing a routine and schedule is essential. These intelligent and energetic dogs thrive on structure and consistency. By implementing a well-defined routine, you can provide your Dachshund with a sense of security and establish clear expectations for behavior. This subchapter will guide you through the process of creating a routine and schedule that will contribute to a well-behaved and happy Dachshund.

The first step in establishing a routine is to determine a daily schedule for your Dachshund. Dogs function best when their day is divided into predictable chunks of time. Consider your Dachshund's needs for feeding, exercise, playtime, training, and rest. Set specific times for each activity and stick to them as closely as possible. Consistency is key when it comes to training, so maintaining the same schedule every day will help reinforce desired behaviors.

Feeding your Dachshund at the same time each day is crucial for maintaining their health and preventing digestive issues. Create a designated feeding area and establish a feeding routine that works for both you and your pet. Be sure to provide a balanced and nutritious diet that meets their specific needs. Consult with your veterinarian to determine the best diet plan for your Dachshund.

Exercise is vital for a Dachshund's physical and mental well-being. Incorporating regular exercise into their daily routine will help burn off excess energy and prevent behavioral problems. Plan daily walks or play sessions to ensure your Dachshund gets the exercise they need. Remember to tailor the intensity and duration of exercise to your Dachshund's age, health, and energy level.

Training sessions should be integrated into your Dachshund's routine. These intelligent dogs are eager to please, and consistent training will help reinforce good behavior and discourage undesirable habits. Allocate specific times for training sessions, and be patient and consistent in your approach. Positive reinforcement techniques, such as treats and praise, work best with Dachshunds.

Lastly, ensure your Dachshund has designated times for rest and relaxation. These small dogs can be prone to back problems, so providing a comfortable and quiet space for them to rest is crucial. Create a cozy bed or crate area where your Dachshund can retreat to when they need downtime.

By establishing a routine and schedule for your Dachshund, you are setting them up for success. Consistency and structure will not only make training easier but also contribute to a well-balanced and contented pet. Remember to consider your Dachshund's individual needs when creating their routine and schedule, and be flexible enough to make adjustments as necessary. With dedication and patience, you'll soon have a happy and well-trained Dachshund by your side.

Understanding Positive Reinforcement and Reward-Based Training

As a pet owner, you want the best for your beloved Dachshund. Training plays a crucial role in shaping their behavior and ensuring a happy and well-adjusted canine companion. In this subchapter, we will explore the concept of positive reinforcement and reward-based training, which are highly effective methods for training your Dachshund.

Positive reinforcement focuses on rewarding desired behaviors rather than punishing unwanted ones. This methodology is based on the belief that dogs learn best through positive experiences and rewards. When your Dachshund performs a desired behavior, such as sitting on command or walking nicely on a leash, you can reinforce it by providing a reward, such as treats, praise, or playtime. This positive reinforcement strengthens the association between the behavior and the reward, making it more likely to be repeated in the future.

Reward-based training goes hand in hand with positive reinforcement. It involves using rewards as motivators to encourage your Dachshund to behave in a certain way. These rewards can be anything that your dog finds enjoyable, such as treats, toys, or even verbal praise. By associating these rewards with specific behaviors, you can effectively teach your Dachshund what is expected of them.

One of the key benefits of positive reinforcement and reward-based training is that it creates a positive and enjoyable learning experience for your Dachshund. By focusing on rewards rather than punishment, you build a strong bond of trust and cooperation with your furry friend. This approach also encourages your Dachshund to think and problem-solve, as they learn to associate their actions with positive outcomes.

To effectively use positive reinforcement and reward-based training with your Dachshund, it is important to identify the rewards that motivate them the most. Every dog is unique, so experiment with different types of rewards to find what works best for your Dachshund. Additionally, consistency and timing are crucial. Ensure that you reward your Dachshund immediately after they exhibit the desired behavior, as this will reinforce the connection between the action and the reward.

In conclusion, positive reinforcement and reward-based training are highly effective methods for training your Dachshund. By focusing on rewarding desired behaviors rather than punishing unwanted ones, you create a positive learning experience for your furry friend. This approach not only strengthens the bond between you and your Dachshund but also encourages them to become well-behaved and obedient companions. So, grab some treats, get ready to shower your Dachshund with praise, and embark on an exciting training journey that will bring you closer to your furry companion.

CHAPTER 3: BASIC DACHSHUND TRAINING COMMANDS

This chapter introduces the core of Dachshund training: basic commands. Essential for everyday interaction and control, these commands form the cornerstone of your Dachshund's obedience and behavior. We'll cover how to effectively teach commands like 'sit', 'stay', 'come', and 'heel', using step-by-step methods tailored for your Dachshund's learning style. Emphasizing patience and consistency, this chapter guides you through shaping your Dachshund's basic obedience, ensuring a well-mannered and responsive companion.

Teaching Your Dachshund to Sit

One of the fundamental commands that every pet owner should teach their Dachshund is the "sit" command. Teaching your Dachshund to sit not only helps establish a clear line of communication between you and your furry friend but also forms the foundation for other essential commands.

To start the training process, find a quiet and distraction-free area in your home where you and your Dachshund can focus. Have some small and tasty treats handy as positive reinforcement is key to successful training. The next step is to get your Dachshund's attention. Call their name and make eye contact, ensuring they are fully engaged with you.

Hold a treat close to your Dachshund's nose and slowly move it upward, towards their head. As their nose follows the treat, their natural response will be to lower their rear end to the ground. When their bottom touches the floor, say the word "sit" in a clear and firm tone, and immediately give them the treat as a reward. Repeat this process several times, consistently using the command word and rewarding them each time they sit correctly.

It's important to keep training sessions short and frequent, as Dachshunds have a relatively short attention span. Aim for five to ten-minute sessions, two to three times a day, to ensure they stay engaged and focused. As your Dachshund begins to understand the command, gradually reduce the frequency of treats, rewarding them intermittently instead. This will help them associate sitting with positive reinforcement rather than solely relying on treats.

Remember to always stay patient and consistent during the training process. Each dog learns at their own pace, so do not get discouraged if your Dachshund takes longer to grasp the concept. Additionally, avoid using physical force or punishment, as this can create fear and hinder the learning process.

Once your Dachshund has mastered the "sit" command, you can move on to more advanced training, such as "stay" or "lie down." The key is to build upon the foundation of basic commands, gradually expanding your Dachshund's repertoire of skills.

By teaching your Dachshund to sit, you are not only enhancing their obedience but also strengthening the bond between you and your furry companion. Remember, patience, consistency, and positive reinforcement are the keys to successful training.

Training Your Dachshund to Stay

One of the most important commands you can teach your Dachshund is the "Stay" command. This command helps ensure their safety and the safety of those around them. It is an essential skill that every pet owner should prioritize when training their Dachshund. In this subchapter, we will discuss the step-by-step process of training your Dachshund to stay.

First and foremost, it is crucial to establish a strong foundation of basic obedience commands such as "Sit" and "Stay" before proceeding with advanced training. Once your Dachshund has mastered these commands, you can begin training them to stay for longer periods.

Start by selecting a quiet, distraction-free area for training sessions. Begin with short durations and gradually increase the time as your Dachshund becomes more comfortable with the command. Use positive reinforcement techniques such as treats, praises, and gentle petting to reward your Dachshund for staying in place.

To begin the training, give the command "Stay" in a firm yet gentle voice while holding your palm up in front of your Dachshund's face. Take a step backward, maintaining eye contact, and wait for a few seconds. If your Dachshund remains in the same spot, praise them and offer a treat as a reward. Repeat this process several times, gradually increasing the distance and duration.

If your Dachshund tries to follow you, calmly return them to the original position without scolding or punishing them. Consistency and patience are key during this training process. Remember to keep the training sessions short and engaging to avoid overwhelming your Dachshund.

Once your Dachshund has mastered staying in place, you can introduce distractions gradually. Start with mild distractions, such as tossing a toy nearby, and gradually progress to more challenging distractions like having someone walk past them. With consistent practice and positive reinforcement, your Dachshund will learn to stay even in the face of various distractions.

Remember, training your Dachshund to stay requires patience, consistency, and positive reinforcement. It is essential to create a positive and rewarding environment for your Dachshund to encourage their progress. By following these steps and dedicating time to training, you will successfully teach your Dachshund to stay, ensuring their safety and enhancing their overall obedience.

Teaching Your Dachshund to Come When Called

One of the most important commands you can teach your Dachshund is to come when called. Not only is this command essential for your dog's safety, but it also ensures a strong bond between you and your pet. In this subchapter, we will guide you through a step-by-step process to successfully train your Dachshund to come when called.

First and foremost, it is crucial to understand the importance of positive reinforcement in training your Dachshund. Dogs respond best to rewards and praise, so always remember to be patient, consistent, and encouraging during the training sessions.

Start by choosing a designated word or phrase to use as your recall command. It could be something like "come" or "here." Make sure to use a confident and enthusiastic tone when giving this command to grab your Dachshund's attention.

Begin the training indoors or in a quiet, enclosed area with minimum distractions. Attach a lightweight leash to your dog's collar and let it drag on the ground. This allows you to gently guide your Dachshund towards you if needed.

Stand a short distance away from your dog and use their name followed by the recall command. For example, "Buddy, come!" Use excited gestures or clap your hands to encourage your dog to come towards you. If your Dachshund starts moving towards you, shower them with praise and offer a tasty treat as a reward. Repeat this exercise several times, gradually increasing the distance between you and your dog.

Once your Dachshund masters the recall command indoors, it's time to move the training outdoors. Start in a secure, fenced area to avoid any potential dangers. Again, keep the leash on for added control. Practice the recall command in various locations, gradually introducing distractions such as other dogs or toys.

Remember to never scold or punish your Dachshund if they don't come immediately. Instead, go back to shorter distances and reinforce the command positively. Consistency is key, so practice this command regularly to reinforce your dog's obedience.

In conclusion, teaching your Dachshund to come when called is an essential part of their training. By following the steps outlined in this subchapter, you can establish a strong recall command that will ensure your dog's safety and strengthen the bond between you and your furry companion. Happy training!

Walking on a Leash: Loose Leash Walking Techniques

Walking on a leash is an essential skill for any dog, including Dachshunds. Not only does it provide exercise and mental stimulation, but it also ensures the safety of your furry friend. However, many pet owners struggle with their Dachshunds pulling and tugging on the leash, turning a pleasant walk into a frustrating experience. In this subchapter, we will explore effective loose leash walking techniques specifically tailored for Dachshunds.

1. Establish a Positive Association: Begin by associating the leash with positive experiences. Let your Dachshund sniff and explore the leash before attaching it. Offer treats and praise to create a positive connection, reinforcing the idea that the leash is not a restriction but a gateway to enjoyable experiences.

2. Start Indoors: Before venturing outside, practice loose leash walking in a controlled environment. Attach the leash and allow your Dachshund to wander around freely while maintaining a loose leash. Reward them with treats and praise for walking calmly beside you.

3. Use Proper Equipment: Ensure you have the right equipment for your Dachshund's size and needs. A harness is recommended over a collar to prevent strain on their delicate necks. Choose a sturdy, comfortable leash that allows for easy control.

4. Be Consistent: Consistency is key in leash training. Use verbal cues like "heel" or "walk" consistently to communicate your expectations. Reinforce positive behavior with rewards and redirect unwanted behavior by stopping or changing direction.

5. Practice Short Sessions: Dachshunds have short attention spans, so keep training sessions brief and frequent. Aim for 10 to 15-minute sessions several times a day, gradually increasing the duration as your Dachshund becomes more comfortable with loose leash walking.

6. Be Patient and Persistent: Leash training takes time and patience. Your Dachshund won't become a perfect walker overnight, so don't get discouraged. Celebrate small victories and remain persistent in your training efforts.

7. Seek Professional Help if Needed: If you find that your Dachshund is particularly stubborn or resistant to leash training, don't hesitate to seek professional assistance. A qualified dog trainer can provide personalized guidance and address any specific issues you may be facing.

Remember, walking on a leash is a learned skill for your Dachshund. With consistent training, positive reinforcement, and patience, you can transform your walks into enjoyable bonding experiences. So, grab your leash, put on your Dachshund's harness, and embark on the journey of loose leash walking together!

CHAPTER 4: HOUSEBREAKING AND CRATE TRAINING

Housebreaking and crate training are fundamental for a harmonious living situation with your Dachshund. This chapter addresses the effective techniques to house-train your pet, dealing with common challenges and setting a routine for success. We also delve into crate training, showing you how to create a positive and safe space for your Dachshund, crucial for their sense of security and your peace of mind. Practical, compassionate approaches are emphasized to make these essential training aspects stress-free and successful.

Understanding the Importance of Housebreaking

Housebreaking, also known as potty training, is a crucial aspect of training for any pet owner, especially those with Dachshunds. As a pet owner, it is your responsibility to teach your furry friend appropriate bathroom behavior, and housebreaking is the key to achieving this.

Housebreaking your Dachshund is essential for several reasons. Firstly, it promotes a clean and hygienic living environment for both you and your pet. No one wants to live in a house filled with unpleasant odors and unsightly messes. By training your Dachshund to relieve themselves in designated areas, you can maintain a clean and fresh-smelling home.

Secondly, housebreaking helps establish a routine and structure for your Dachshund. Dogs thrive on routine, and having a set schedule for bathroom breaks can make them feel more secure and confident. It also allows you to anticipate when your pet needs to go, preventing accidents and further reinforcing the bond between you and your furry companion.

Additionally, successful housebreaking can prevent destructive behavior. When Dachshunds are not properly trained, they may resort to relieving themselves indoors, causing damage to your furniture, carpets, and belongings. By teaching your Dachshund appropriate bathroom behavior, you can avoid these destructive habits and save yourself from unnecessary frustration and expenses.

Housebreaking is a process that requires patience, consistency, and positive reinforcement. It is important to establish a designated potty area in your home and consistently take your Dachshund to that spot. Rewarding them with praise, treats, or playtime when they eliminate in the appropriate area will reinforce the desired behavior.

Furthermore, understanding the signs that your Dachshund needs to relieve themselves is crucial. Common signs include restlessness, sniffing, circling, or suddenly leaving the room. By being attentive and recognizing these cues, you can prevent accidents and guide your Dachshund to the designated potty area.

Remember, accidents are bound to happen during the housebreaking process. It is essential to remain patient and avoid punishing your Dachshund for accidents. Instead, focus on positive reinforcement and redirecting their behavior to the designated potty area.

In conclusion, housebreaking is a fundamental aspect of training for Dachshund owners. By understanding the importance of housebreaking and implementing consistent training methods, you can create a clean, structured, and harmonious living environment for both you and your beloved pet.

Establishing a Housebreaking Routine

Housebreaking a dachshund can be a challenging task, but with the right approach and consistent training, you can teach your furry friend to do their business in the appropriate place. This subchapter will guide you through the process of establishing a housebreaking routine that will help your dachshund become a well-behaved and house-trained pet.

The key to successful housebreaking lies in consistency and patience. Dachshunds are intelligent dogs, but they can be stubborn at times. It's important to remember that accidents will happen, especially during the early stages of training. Stay calm and avoid punishing your dachshund for accidents, as this may create anxiety and hinder their progress.

The first step in establishing a housebreaking routine is to set up a designated potty area for your dachshund. This could be a specific spot in your yard or a pee pad placed indoors. Take your dachshund to this area after meals, naps, or playtime, as well as first thing in the morning and before bedtime. Be patient and wait for them to eliminate, rewarding them with praise and treats when they do.

Another important aspect of housebreaking is to establish a consistent feeding schedule. Regular mealtimes will help regulate your dachshund's digestive system, making it easier for you to predict when they need to go outside. Avoid leaving food out all day and instead offer meals at specific times. This will also help you monitor their water intake, reducing the chances of accidents.

Supervision is crucial during the housebreaking process. Whenever you can't directly supervise your dachshund, confine them to a small, safe area using a crate or baby gate. This will prevent accidents and give them a clear understanding of their boundaries. When you are able to supervise, keep a close eye on your dachshund's behavior and body language. If they start sniffing or circling, it's a sign that they need to go outside.

Consistency is key when housebreaking a dachshund. Stick to your routine even on weekends or when you have a busy day. This will help your dachshund learn faster and reinforce their understanding of where they should eliminate. Remember to always reward good behavior and be patient with your furry friend.

With a well-established housebreaking routine, you can enjoy a clean and pleasant home environment while having a happy and well-trained dachshund companion.

Introducing Crate Training to Your Dachshund

Crate training is an essential aspect of training your Dachshund. It provides them with a safe and comfortable space of their own, and helps in preventing undesirable behaviors such as destructive chewing and soiling in the house. In this subchapter, we will guide you through the process of introducing crate training to your Dachshund and make it a positive experience for both you and your furry friend.

The first step in crate training is choosing the right crate for your Dachshund. Make sure it is big enough for them to stand, turn around, and lie down comfortably. Opt for a crate with a sturdy build and a secure door. You can also make the crate cozy by adding a soft blanket or a dog bed.

To introduce your Dachshund to the crate, start by placing the crate in a location where your pet spends most of their time. Leave the crate door open and allow your Dachshund to explore it at their own pace. Encourage them with treats or their favorite toys to create a positive association with the crate. Avoid forcing your pet into the crate as it may create a negative experience.

Once your Dachshund starts showing interest in the crate, begin feeding them near the crate. Gradually move their food bowl closer to the crate, eventually placing it inside the crate. This will help them associate the crate with positive experiences like mealtime.

After your Dachshund is comfortable eating inside the crate, you can start closing the door for short periods of time. Stay nearby and provide reassurance if they become anxious. Gradually increase the duration of time spent in the crate, making sure to reward your pet for their good behavior.

It's important to note that crate training should never be used as a form of punishment. The crate should always be a positive and safe space for your Dachshund. Never leave your pet in the crate for extended periods of time, as they need regular exercise and social interaction.

Consistency is key when crate training your Dachshund. Stick to a routine and use the crate for short periods throughout the day. With patience and positive reinforcement, your Dachshund will eventually see the crate as their own personal den, providing them with comfort and security.

In conclusion, crate training is an effective way to provide a safe and comfortable space for your Dachshund. By following the steps outlined in this subchapter, you can successfully introduce crate training to your pet and enjoy a well-behaved and contented Dachshund. Remember to always approach crate training with patience, love, and positive reinforcement.

Dealing with Accidents and Troubleshooting Housebreaking Issues

Accidents happen, especially when it comes to housebreaking your Dachshund. However, with patience, consistency, and the right techniques, you can successfully train your furry friend to become housebroken. In this chapter, we will discuss some common housebreaking issues that pet owners face and provide you with effective solutions to address them.

One of the most common issues is when your Dachshund continues to have accidents even after you have been diligently training them. This can be frustrating, but it's important not to lose hope. Firstly, make sure you are providing your Dachshund with ample opportunities to relieve themselves outside. Take them out first thing in the morning, after meals, and before bedtime. Additionally, establish a regular feeding schedule to predict when they will need to go.

If accidents still occur, it's crucial not to punish your Dachshund. Instead, redirect their behavior and reinforce positive habits. When you catch them in the act of having an accident, say a firm "no" and immediately take them outside. Once they finish their business outside, praise and reward them with treats or verbal affirmations. This positive reinforcement will help them associate going outside with positive experiences.

Another common issue is when your Dachshund starts to regress in their housebreaking training. This can happen due to various reasons, such as changes in routine, stress, or medical issues. If regression occurs, it's essential to evaluate any changes that may have triggered it. Reestablish a consistent routine and monitor your Dachshund's behavior for signs of stress or discomfort. If necessary, consult with a veterinarian to rule out any underlying health issues.

In some cases, accidents may happen because your Dachshund isn't fully grasping the concept of housebreaking. To prevent accidents, consider using a crate or a confined area when you can't supervise your Dachshund. Dogs naturally avoid soiling their sleeping area, so this will help them develop bladder control. Gradually increase their freedom as they become more reliable in their housebreaking skills.

Remember, housebreaking a Dachshund takes time and patience. Consistency is key, so be prepared for setbacks along the way. With proper training techniques and a positive attitude, you can successfully overcome housebreaking issues and enjoy a harmonious relationship with your Dachshund.

In conclusion, this subchapter has covered common accidents and troubleshooting housebreaking issues that you may encounter during the training process. By implementing the techniques mentioned, you can address accidents effectively and help your Dachshund become fully housebroken. Stay dedicated to the training process, and soon enough, you'll have a well-trained and obedient Dachshund that you can proudly call your own.

CHAPTER 5:
SOCIALIZING YOUR
DACHSHUND

A well-socialized Dachshund is a confident and happy dog. This chapter focuses on the importance of socializing your pet with other animals, people, and various environments. We provide strategies for introducing your Dachshund to new experiences, reducing fear and aggression, and ensuring they develop into well-adjusted adults. The chapter offers insights on handling different social scenarios, equipping you to guide your Dachshund through the world with confidence and ease.

The Importance of Early Socialization

As a pet owner, one of the most crucial aspects of training your Dachshund is early socialization. This process involves exposing your furry friend to a wide range of people, animals, and environments during their critical developmental phase, which is typically between the ages of 3 to 14 weeks. The significance of early socialization cannot be overstated, as it lays the foundation for a well-behaved and confident Dachshund.

Socialization plays a pivotal role in shaping your Dachshund's behavior and temperament. By exposing them to various stimuli early on, you can help prevent behavioral issues such as fear, anxiety, and aggression in adulthood. Dachshunds are known for their loyal and protective nature, but without proper socialization, they may become overly wary or even aggressive towards strangers or other animals. Early exposure to different individuals, including children, adults, and other pets, will teach your Dachshund to be comfortable and accepting of different personalities and species.

Furthermore, early socialization aids in building your Dachshund's confidence. By exposing them to new environments, sounds, and experiences, you can help them become more adaptable and less prone to stress or anxiety. This is especially important for Dachshunds, as their small size may make them more vulnerable to fear-based behaviors if not properly socialized. Taking your Dachshund for walks in various locations, allowing them to explore different surfaces, and introducing them to different sights and sounds will contribute to their overall confidence and well-being.

It is crucial to note that socialization should be a positive and gradual process. Start by introducing your Dachshund to new experiences in a controlled environment, ensuring they feel safe and supported. Use positive reinforcement techniques such as treats, praise, and play to reward their calm and relaxed behavior during these encounters. Gradually increase the level of difficulty by exposing them to more challenging situations, always monitoring their reactions and adjusting accordingly.

In conclusion, early socialization is an essential aspect of training your Dachshund. By providing them with a wide range of positive experiences during their critical developmental period, you can shape their behavior and temperament for a lifetime. Remember, a well-socialized Dachshund is more likely to be friendly, confident, and well-adjusted, making them a joy to have as a pet. So, invest the time and effort in socializing your Dachshund early on, and you'll reap the rewards of a happy and well-behaved companion.

Introducing Your Dachshund to Other Animals

As a pet owner and lover of dachshunds, it's important to ensure that your furry friend is well-socialized and gets along with other animals. Whether you have cats, dogs, or even smaller pets like rabbits or birds, introducing your dachshund to other animals can be a smooth and successful process with the right approach. In this subchapter, we will provide you with expert tips and guidance on how to introduce your dachshund to other animals, ensuring a harmonious and safe environment for everyone in your household.

First and foremost, it's crucial to remember that every animal has its own unique personality and temperament. When introducing your dachshund to another animal, it's essential to take things slow and allow them to get to know each other gradually. This will help to prevent any potential conflicts or negative experiences.

Start by allowing your dachshund and the other animal to sniff each other's scents without direct physical contact. This can be done by swapping blankets or toys between them. By familiarizing themselves with each other's scent, they can become more comfortable in each other's presence.

Next, you can arrange a controlled meeting between the animals in a neutral and familiar space. This allows both animals to feel more at ease and reduces the likelihood of territorial behavior. Keep your dachshund on a leash during this initial meeting, and closely monitor their interactions.

Positive reinforcement plays a crucial role in introducing your dachshund to other animals. Reward your dachshund for calm and friendly behavior towards the other animal, using treats or verbal praise. This will reinforce positive associations and encourage your dachshund to continue exhibiting good behavior.

Be patient and understanding throughout the process. Some animals may take longer to adjust and feel comfortable around each other. It's important not to rush the introduction and to create a safe environment for both animals. If necessary, seek professional guidance from a certified dog trainer or animal behaviorist who specializes in inter-animal introductions.

Remember, not all animals will become best friends, but with proper introduction techniques and ongoing socialization, you can foster a peaceful coexistence between your dachshund and other animals in your household. By following these guidelines and being attentive to their needs, you'll be well on your way to creating a harmonious and happy family dynamic for all your beloved pets.

In conclusion, introducing your dachshund to other animals requires patience, positive reinforcement, and a gradual approach. By following the expert tips provided in this subchapter, you can ensure that your dachshund becomes a well-adjusted and friendly companion to all the animals in your home.

Exposing Your Dachshund to Different Environments

As pet owners, we want our Dachshunds to be well-rounded and adaptable to various environments. Exposing your Dachshund to different environments is not only essential for their overall development but also plays a crucial role in their training journey. In this subchapter, we will delve into why it is important to expose your Dachshund to different environments and provide you with practical tips to make this process easier.

Dachshunds are known for their intelligence and loyalty, but they can also be prone to anxiety and fearfulness if not properly socialized. By exposing your Dachshund to a variety of environments, you can help them become more confident, adaptable, and less prone to anxious behaviors. This exposure will not only benefit their overall well-being but will also make training them much easier.

One of the best ways to expose your Dachshund to different environments is through regular outings. Take your furry companion on trips to the park, beach, or even a bustling city street. Gradually introduce them to new sights, smells, and sounds, allowing them to become familiar with different stimuli. Begin with shorter outings and gradually increase the duration and intensity of the experiences. This gradual approach will help your Dachshund build positive associations with new environments.

Socialization with other dogs and people is another crucial aspect of exposing your Dachshund to different environments. Organize playdates with other dogs, enroll them in obedience classes, or take them to dog-friendly events. Encourage interactions with a variety of people, including children and strangers, to help them develop a friendly and confident demeanor.

Additionally, consider exposing your Dachshund to different surfaces, such as grass, sand, or hardwood floors. This exposure will help them become comfortable walking on various terrains. Introduce them to different objects, such as stairs, ramps, or even elevators, to build their confidence and adaptability.

Always remember to make these experiences positive and rewarding for your Dachshund. Bring their favorite treats or toys along to associate these new environments with positive experiences. Praise and reward them for their bravery and good behavior, reinforcing their confidence.

In conclusion, exposing your Dachshund to different environments is vital for their training and overall well-being. By gradually introducing them to new experiences, people, and surfaces, you can help them become adaptable, confident, and less prone to anxiety. Embrace the journey of exploration with your Dachshund, and watch as they blossom into a well-rounded and happy companion.

Handling Fear and Aggression in Social Situations

As pet owners, we understand the importance of socializing our beloved Dachshunds. However, sometimes our furry friends can exhibit fear or aggression in social situations, causing stress for both the dog and owner. In this subchapter, we will dive into effective strategies for managing and overcoming fear and aggression in social settings, ensuring a well-adjusted and confident Dachshund.

First and foremost, it is crucial to identify the triggers that cause fear or aggression in your Dachshund. Is it unfamiliar people, other dogs, or specific environments? Once you have pinpointed the triggers, you can gradually expose your dog to them in a controlled and positive manner. This process, known as desensitization, involves gradually increasing exposure to the trigger while pairing it with positive experiences such as treats or playtime. Over time, your Dachshund will associate the trigger with positive outcomes, reducing fear or aggression.

Additionally, counter-conditioning techniques can be highly effective in managing fear and aggression. This method involves redirecting your Dachshund's attention to something positive when they start to exhibit fear or aggression. For example, if your dog becomes anxious when meeting new people, guide their focus onto a favorite toy or treat, distracting them from their fearful emotions.

It is crucial to remain calm and composed during social interactions to avoid reinforcing your dog's fear or aggression. Dogs are incredibly perceptive, and they can sense our emotions. If you become anxious or tense, your Dachshund will pick up on these cues, further exacerbating their own fear or aggression. Instead, model confidence and reassurance, providing a sense of security for your pet.

Seeking professional help from a certified dog trainer or behaviorist can also be beneficial, especially if your Dachshund's fear or aggression is severe or persistent. These experts can provide personalized guidance and training techniques tailored to your dog's specific needs.

Remember, socialization is a lifelong process, and consistency is key. Regular exposure to various social situations and continued positive reinforcement will help your Dachshund build confidence and overcome fear or aggression. By implementing the strategies outlined in this subchapter, you can ensure that your Dachshund becomes a well-rounded and sociable furry companion, bringing joy to both you and those around you.

CHAPTER 6: ADVANCED DACHSHUND TRAINING TECHNIQUES

Building upon basic obedience, this chapter ventures into advanced training techniques to further challenge and engage your Dachshund. We explore more complex commands and tricks, agility training, and specialized training areas like therapy and service work. This chapter is designed to deepen the bond between you and your Dachshund while enhancing their skills and mental stimulation.

Teaching Your Dachshund Advanced Commands

Congratulations on completing the basics of training your Dachshund! Now it's time to take your furry friend's skills to the next level with advanced commands. This subchapter in "Dachshund Survival Guide: How to Train Your Dachshund" will help you unlock your Dachshund's full potential and enhance your bond even further.

Advanced commands not only impress your friends and family but also provide mental stimulation for your Dachshund, keeping them engaged and active. Let's dive into some essential advanced commands that will transform your Dachshund into a well-rounded and obedient companion.

1. "Stay": Training your Dachshund to "stay" is an exercise in self-control for your pet. Begin by ensuring your dog has mastered the "sit" or "down" command. Once in position, introduce the "stay" command with an open palm hand signal. Start by stepping back a small distance, wait a few seconds, then return to your dog and reward them with a treat and praise. Gradually increase the distance and duration, ensuring to return to your dog to reward them, rather than calling them to you. It's important to set your Dachshund up for success by increasing difficulty slowly and practicing in various environments with different levels of distraction.

2. "Leave it": The "leave it" command is crucial for preventing your Dachshund from interacting with potentially harmful objects. Begin by holding a treat in a closed fist and allowing your dog to sniff it. Once they stop sniffing and look away, say "leave it," and give them a different treat from your other hand. Practice this until your Dachshund consistently turns away from the first treat. Then, progress to placing the treat on the floor and covering it with your hand. As your Dachshund gets better at the command, you can try leaving the treat uncovered, rewarding them for obeying the "leave it" command.

3. "Roll over": Teaching your Dachshund to "roll over" is a fun trick. Start with your dog in a 'down' position. Hold a treat near their nose and slowly move it towards their shoulder, encouraging them to lie on their side. Continue moving the treat around their shoulder to their back, guiding them into a full roll. As they complete the roll, say "roll over" and give them the treat. This trick may require some patience and practice, and it's important to keep the training sessions short and fun.

4. "Fetch": "Fetch" is a fantastic way to exercise your Dachshund both mentally and physically. Begin with a toy that your dog is interested in and throw it a short distance. Encourage your dog to go after the toy with an enthusiastic "fetch." When your dog picks up the toy, call them back to you and offer a treat in exchange for the toy. Praise them enthusiastically. As they understand the game, you can gradually increase the distance. If your Dachshund doesn't naturally return the toy, you can train this by using two toys and swapping them each time your dog returns.

5. "Speak" or "Quiet": Training your Dachshund to "speak," or bark on command, and then to be "quiet" is about controlling their natural vocalization. To teach "speak," find a trigger that naturally causes your dog to bark, like a doorbell. When they bark, say "speak," and then reward them. For "quiet," wait for a moment of silence after a bark, say "quiet," and then provide a treat. With repetition, your dog will learn to associate these commands with their barking and silence. Remember to be consistent with your commands and rewards.

Remember, patience and consistency are key when teaching advanced commands. Break down each command into small steps, and practice them in short sessions to prevent your Dachshund from becoming overwhelmed. Always use positive reinforcement, rewarding your Dachshund with treats, praise, and affection.

By teaching your Dachshund advanced commands, you'll not only stimulate their mind but also deepen the bond between you and your beloved pet. So, grab your copy of "Dachshund Survival Guide: How to Train Your Dachshund" and embark on this exciting journey with your Dachshund today!

Dachshund Agility Training

Dachshunds are renowned for their lively and curious nature, making them excellent candidates for agility training. Not only does agility training provide mental stimulation, but it also helps to keep your Dachshund physically fit and healthy. In this subchapter, we will explore the world of Dachshund agility training and provide you with a step-by-step guide to get started.

Agility training involves teaching your Dachshund to navigate through an obstacle course that includes jumps, tunnels, weave poles, and more. It requires a strong bond between you and your pet, as well as patience and consistency in training. The benefits of agility training are numerous, from increased confidence and obedience to improved coordination and problem-solving skills.

Before diving into agility training, it is essential to ensure that your Dachshund is in good health and has received proper obedience training. A visit to the veterinarian will help determine if your dog is physically fit for agility training. Once you have the green light, it's time to begin!

The first step is to introduce your Dachshund to the various agility obstacles gradually. Start with simple commands such as sit, stay, and come, ensuring that your dog understands and obeys them. Once your Dachshund is comfortable with these commands, you can introduce low jumps and tunnels, rewarding your pet for successfully completing each task.

As your Dachshund progresses, you can gradually increase the difficulty level of the obstacles. Teach your dog to weave through poles, balance on a seesaw, and navigate through tire jumps. Remember to use positive reinforcement techniques such as treats and praise to motivate your Dachshund throughout the training process.

Consistency is key in agility training. Set aside regular training sessions, preferably at the same time and place, to help your Dachshund develop a routine. Be patient and understanding, as some dogs may take longer to grasp certain skills than others. Celebrate every small achievement and never punish your Dachshund for mistakes.

In addition to physical training, mental stimulation is crucial for Dachshunds. Incorporate problem-solving games and puzzles into your training routine to challenge your dog's intelligence. This will keep their mind sharp and prevent boredom, leading to a happier and healthier Dachshund.

In conclusion, Dachshund agility training is a fantastic way to bond with your pet and keep them mentally and physically fit. With patience, consistency, and positive reinforcement, you can train your Dachshund to navigate through various agility obstacles. Remember to always prioritize your dog's safety and well-being throughout the training process. Happy training!

Dachshund Obedience Competitions

For pet owners who are passionate about training their Dachshunds, participating in obedience competitions can be an exciting and rewarding experience. These competitions not only showcase the intelligence and capabilities of your four-legged friend but also provide an opportunity to bond and strengthen the relationship between you and your Dachshund.

Obedience competitions are organized events where Dachshunds and their owners can demonstrate their skills and mastery of various commands and exercises. These competitions are divided into different levels, ranging from beginner to advanced, ensuring that every Dachshund can participate regardless of their training experience.

One of the most appealing aspects of obedience competitions is the chance to compete against other Dachshunds and their owners. This friendly competition fosters a sense of camaraderie among pet owners and allows you to learn from others who share a similar passion for training their Dachshunds. It's a fantastic opportunity to exchange training tips, techniques, and even make new friends who understand the unique challenges and joys of raising a Dachshund.

In these competitions, Dachshunds are evaluated based on their performance in a series of exercises, including heeling, recall, sit-stay, down-stay, and more. The judges assess the precision, responsiveness, and overall execution of these commands. The goal is to showcase your Dachshund's ability to perform these exercises with accuracy, speed, and enthusiasm while maintaining a strong connection and focus on you as their handler.

Participating in obedience competitions not only helps you gauge your Dachshund's progress in their training journey but also serves as a motivational tool to continuously improve your training techniques. The feedback and constructive criticism provided by the judges can offer valuable insights into areas where you and your Dachshund can continue to grow and excel.

Remember, obedience competitions are not just about winning trophies or accolades; they are about building a stronger bond and enhancing the overall well-being of your Dachshund. The time spent training and preparing for these competitions will further deepen your understanding of your Dachshund's unique personality and capabilities.

So, if you are a pet owner who is passionate about training your Dachshund and are looking for a way to showcase their skills while having fun, consider participating in obedience competitions. They offer an incredible platform to celebrate the intelligence, agility, and obedience of your beloved Dachshund while connecting with like-minded individuals who share the same love for this charming breed.

Tricks and Games to Stimulate Your Dachshund's Mind

Keeping your Dachshund mentally stimulated is just as important as physical exercise. These intelligent and curious dogs thrive on mental challenges, and engaging their minds can help prevent boredom and destructive behaviors. In this subchapter, we will explore some fun and effective tricks and games that will keep your Dachshund's mind sharp and entertained.

1. Hide-and-Seek: This classic game is not only fun, but it also taps into your Dachshund's natural hunting instincts. Start by hiding treats or toys around the house and encouraging your Dachshund to find them. As they become more skilled, you can increase the difficulty level by hiding the items in harder-to-reach places.

2. Puzzle Toys: Invest in interactive puzzle toys that require your Dachshund to solve a problem to access their treats. These toys come in various shapes and sizes, offering different levels of difficulty. They are fantastic mental workout tools that will challenge your Dachshund's problem-solving skills and keep them entertained for hours.

3. Teach New Tricks: Dachshunds are intelligent and eager to please, making them quick learners. Teach them new tricks like "sit," "stay," "rollover," or even more advanced tricks like "fetch the newspaper." Not only will this stimulate their minds, but it will also strengthen your bond with your furry friend.

4. Obstacle Courses: Set up a mini-obstacle course in your backyard or living room using everyday objects like cones, hula hoops, and tunnels. Guide your Dachshund through the course, encouraging them to jump, crawl, and navigate their way through. This activity will challenge their physical abilities and engage their problem-solving skills.

5. Food Dispensing Toys: Invest in food dispensing toys that require your Dachshund to work for their meals. These toys can be filled with kibble or treats and have various mechanisms that make it challenging for your dog to access the food. This not only provides mental stimulation but also slows down their eating pace, reducing the risk of digestive issues.

Remember, mental stimulation should be a regular part of your Dachshund's routine. By incorporating these tricks and games into your training sessions and playtime, you can ensure that your Dachshund is not only physically fit but also mentally fulfilled. A stimulated Dachshund is a happy and well-behaved companion, ready to take on any challenge that comes their way.

CHAPTER 7: SOLVING COMMON DACHSHUND BEHAVIOR PROBLEMS

In this chapter, we address common behavioral issues specific to Dachshunds, such as separation anxiety, excessive barking, digging, and chewing. Offering practical solutions and expert advice, we guide you through understanding and modifying these behaviors. This chapter is key to ensuring a well-behaved Dachshund and a harmonious home environment.

Separation Anxiety and Excessive Barking

One of the biggest challenges that pet owners face when training a Dachshund is dealing with separation anxiety and excessive barking. These issues can be quite common in this breed, but with the right approach and techniques, you can help your furry friend overcome these behaviors. In this subchapter, we will discuss the causes of separation anxiety and excessive barking in Dachshunds and provide practical tips to address these problems effectively.

Separation anxiety occurs when dogs become anxious or stressed when left alone. Dachshunds are known for their strong attachment to their owners, making them more prone to this condition. Signs of separation anxiety may include destructive behavior, excessive barking, pacing, or even soiling in the house. To help your Dachshund cope with this anxiety, it is essential to gradually acclimate them to being alone. Start by leaving them alone for short periods and gradually increase the duration. Provide them with engaging toys or treat-dispensing puzzles to keep them occupied.

Excessive barking is another common problem among Dachshunds. These little dogs have a big voice and can be quite vocal. Excessive barking can be triggered by various factors, including boredom, fear, or territorial behavior. To address this issue, it is important to identify the underlying cause. Ensure that your Dachshund receives enough physical and mental stimulation through regular exercise and interactive playtime. Teaching them the "quiet" command and rewarding them when they stop barking can also be beneficial. Additionally, consider using positive reinforcement techniques to redirect their attention and reward them for calm behavior.

In some cases, separation anxiety and excessive barking may require professional help. If your Dachshund's behavior does not improve despite your best efforts, consult a professional dog trainer or behaviorist who can provide specialized guidance and support.

Remember, training a Dachshund takes time and patience. By understanding the causes of separation anxiety and excessive barking and implementing the appropriate training methods, you can help your furry friend become a well-behaved and happy companion.

In conclusion, separation anxiety and excessive barking are common challenges faced by Dachshund owners. However, with the right approach, these behaviors can be effectively addressed. Gradual acclimation to being alone, providing mental and physical stimulation, and using positive reinforcement techniques are key strategies to tackle these issues. By following these tips and seeking professional help when needed, you can ensure that your Dachshund is a well-rounded and contented family member.

Dachshund Digging and Chewing Behaviors

Dachshunds are known for their adorable appearance and loyal nature, but they also have some behaviors that can be challenging for pet owners to handle. Two of these common behaviors are digging and chewing. In this subchapter, we will explore why Dachshunds engage in these behaviors and provide effective strategies for training them out of it.

Digging is a natural instinct for Dachshunds, as they were originally bred for hunting small game. However, in a domestic setting, this behavior can be destructive and frustrating. Understanding the root cause of digging is essential in addressing the issue. Dachshunds may dig out of boredom, seeking attention, or to escape from a confined space. By providing mental and physical stimulation through regular exercise, interactive toys, and engaging training sessions, you can reduce their urge to dig. Additionally, creating a designated digging area in your yard can redirect their digging instinct and save your flower beds.

Chewing is another behavior that Dachshund owners often grapple with. Puppies, in particular, tend to chew to alleviate teething discomfort. However, adult Dachshunds may continue this behavior due to anxiety, boredom, or lack of proper chew toys. To discourage chewing, it is crucial to provide appropriate chew toys that are durable and safe for your Dachshund to gnaw on. Regularly rotate the toys to keep them interesting and prevent them from becoming bored. Additionally, positive reinforcement training techniques can be employed to redirect their chewing behavior towards acceptable items.

It is essential to note that punishment is not an effective method for curbing digging and chewing behaviors in Dachshunds. Instead, positive reinforcement techniques such as praise, treats, and gentle redirection should be utilized. Consistency and patience are key when training your Dachshund, as it may take time for them to break these habits.

By understanding the reasons behind Dachshund digging and chewing behaviors and implementing the appropriate training techniques, you can successfully overcome these challenges. With dedication and consistency, you can ensure that your Dachshund becomes a well-behaved and contented member of your family.

Aggression and Dominance Issues

Dealing with aggression and dominance issues in your Dachshund can be a challenging and sometimes frustrating experience. However, understanding the root causes of these behaviors and implementing the right training techniques can help you effectively address these issues and maintain a harmonious relationship with your furry friend.

Aggression can manifest in various ways, such as growling, barking, biting, or even lunging. While it's important to remember that aggression is a natural instinct in dogs, it is essential to address it promptly to prevent any potential harm to you, your Dachshund, or others.

One common cause of aggression and dominance issues in Dachshunds is a lack of socialization. If your Dachshund hasn't been exposed to different people, animals, or environments during their critical socialization period (between 3 and 14 weeks), they may become fearful or defensive when confronted with new situations. To combat this, gradually introduce your Dachshund to new experiences, people, and animals, ensuring positive interactions and rewards for calm behavior.

Another factor that can contribute to aggression is improper training and inconsistent boundaries. Dachshunds are intelligent and independent dogs, and without clear rules and consistent guidance, they may develop dominant behaviors. Establishing yourself as the pack leader through positive reinforcement training techniques, such as reward-based training and consistency, will help your Dachshund understand their place in the hierarchy and reduce their aggressive tendencies.

Additionally, it's crucial to address any underlying health issues that may contribute to aggression. Pain, discomfort, or hormonal imbalances can cause behavioral changes in dogs. Regular veterinary check-ups and open communication with your veterinarian can help identify and treat any medical conditions that may be affecting your Dachshund's behavior.

In severe cases of aggression, seeking professional help from a certified dog trainer or behaviorist is highly recommended. These experts can assess your Dachshund's behavior, identify triggers, and tailor a training plan to address their specific issues effectively.

Remember, aggression and dominance issues in Dachshunds can be challenging, but with patience, consistency, and proper training, you can help your furry companion become a well-mannered and balanced member of your family.

Dealing with Fear and Anxiety in Dachshunds

As pet owners, we understand that our furry friends can sometimes experience fear and anxiety. Dachshunds, with their unique personalities, are no exception. In this subchapter, we will explore effective strategies to help you address and manage fear and anxiety in your beloved Dachshund.

Firstly, it is crucial to identify the signs of fear and anxiety in your Dachshund. These may include trembling, excessive barking or whining, hiding, aggression, or even destructive behavior. Once you notice these signs, it's time to take action.

One of the most effective ways to alleviate fear and anxiety in Dachshunds is through desensitization and counter-conditioning. This involves exposing your pet gradually to the source of their fear or anxiety while providing positive reinforcement. For example, if your Dachshund is afraid of loud noises, you can play recorded sounds at a low volume and reward your dog with treats and praise. Gradually increase the volume over time while continuing to reward positive behavior. This method helps your Dachshund associate the previously feared stimulus with positive experiences, reducing their anxiety.

Another useful technique is creating a safe space for your Dachshund. Set up a comfortable and secure area in your home where your pet can retreat when feeling anxious. This could be a crate, a specific room, or even a designated corner with their favorite toys and blankets. Encourage your Dachshund to use this space whenever they feel overwhelmed, providing them with a sense of security and control.

Regular exercise and mental stimulation are also essential in managing fear and anxiety. Dachshunds are energetic dogs that require both physical and mental challenges to stay balanced. Engage in daily walks, playtime, and puzzle toys to keep your Dachshund's mind and body active. A tired dog is a happy and relaxed dog, less prone to anxiety.

In some cases, seeking professional help from a veterinarian or dog behaviorist may be necessary, especially if your Dachshund's fear and anxiety are severe or persistent. They can provide additional guidance and recommend appropriate medications or therapies to assist in managing your pet's condition.

Remember, patience and consistency are key when dealing with fear and anxiety in Dachshunds. By understanding their unique needs and implementing the right strategies, you can help your furry friend feel safe, loved, and confident in any situation.

CHAPTER 8: MAINTAINING A HEALTHY DACHSHUND LIFESTYLE

The focus of this chapter is on the overall well-being of your Dachshund, covering aspects like proper nutrition, exercise, grooming, and regular veterinary care. We provide comprehensive advice to keep your Dachshund physically fit, mentally sharp, and healthy, which is vital for a happy and long-lasting companionship.

Proper Nutrition and Diet for Dachshunds

As a pet owner, one of the most important aspects of caring for your Dachshund is ensuring they receive proper nutrition and maintain a healthy diet. A balanced diet plays a crucial role in their overall well-being, growth, and development. In this subchapter, we will explore the nutritional needs of Dachshunds and provide you with guidance on how to choose the right food for your furry friend.

Dachshunds are a unique breed with specific dietary requirements. Being a small breed, they have a relatively high metabolism, which means they need a diet that is rich in nutrients and energy. It is recommended to feed your

Dachshund a high-quality commercial dog food that is specially formulated for small breeds. Look for a brand that includes real meat as the primary ingredient, as this ensures they receive the necessary protein for muscle development.

Additionally, Dachshunds are prone to obesity, which can lead to various health issues, including joint problems and diabetes. Therefore, it is crucial to monitor their food intake and avoid overfeeding. Follow the recommended feeding guidelines provided by the manufacturer, and adjust the portion sizes based on your Dachshund's age, activity level, and overall health.

When it comes to treats, choose healthy options that are low in fat and calories. Avoid giving them table scraps or human food, as this can lead to weight gain and digestive issues. Instead, opt for treats that are specifically designed for small breed dogs and offer nutritional benefits.

Furthermore, it is essential to provide your Dachshund with fresh water at all times. Hydration is crucial for their overall health, especially since Dachshunds are prone to urinary tract problems. Make sure to clean their water bowl daily to prevent bacteria buildup.

While commercial dog food is convenient and provides the necessary nutrients, some pet owners prefer to prepare homemade meals for their Dachshunds. If you choose this route, consult with a veterinarian or a canine nutritionist to ensure you are meeting all their nutritional requirements.

In conclusion, proper nutrition and diet play a vital role in the training, growth, and overall health of your Dachshund. By feeding them a well-balanced diet, monitoring their food intake, and providing them with fresh water, you can ensure that your Dachshund leads a happy and healthy life.

Exercise and Physical Activity Recommendations

As a pet owner, it is essential to understand the importance of exercise and physical activity for your Dachshund. Regular exercise not only helps maintain a healthy weight but also promotes mental stimulation and overall well-being. In this subchapter, we will delve into the exercise and physical activity recommendations specifically tailored for Dachshunds, ensuring that you provide them with the right amount and type of exercise they need.

Dachshunds are known for their short legs and long bodies, which can make them more susceptible to certain health issues, particularly spinal problems. Therefore, it is crucial to strike a balance between exercising and protecting their delicate backs. Low-impact exercises such as walking, swimming, and gentle play are ideal for Dachshunds. Avoid activities that involve jumping or excessive running, as these can put unnecessary strain on their backs.

To keep your Dachshund in good physical shape, aim for at least 30 minutes to an hour of exercise every day. Break it up into shorter sessions if needed, as it can be easier for them to handle. Regular walks are a great way to meet their exercise requirements while also providing mental stimulation through sniffing and exploring their surroundings. Consider using a harness instead of a collar to reduce strain on their necks during walks.

In addition to daily walks, engaging your Dachshund in interactive playtime can be highly beneficial. Puzzle toys and treat-dispensing toys are excellent choices to keep them mentally stimulated while burning off excess energy. These activities not only provide exercise but also help prevent destructive behaviors that can arise from boredom.

It's important to note that each Dachshund is unique, and their exercise needs may vary. Factors such as age, weight, and overall health should be taken into consideration when designing an exercise routine. Consult with your veterinarian to ensure you are providing the right amount and type of exercise for your individual Dachshund.

Remember that exercise is just one aspect of your Dachshund's overall well-being. Alongside physical activity, a nutritious diet, proper training, and regular veterinary check-ups are equally important for their health and happiness. By incorporating these recommendations into your pet care routine, you can ensure that your Dachshund leads a well-balanced and fulfilling life.

Grooming Tips for Dachshunds

Proper grooming is essential for maintaining the health and appearance of your beloved Dachshund. Their unique coat and body structure require special attention to keep them looking and feeling their best. In this subchapter, we will discuss grooming tips specifically tailored for Dachshunds, helping you ensure your furry friend stays clean, comfortable, and happy.

1. Brushing: Dachshunds have a short, smooth coat, but they still shed regularly. To minimize shedding and keep their coat healthy, regular brushing is necessary. Use a soft-bristle brush or a grooming mitt to remove loose hairs, dirt, and debris. Brushing also helps distribute natural oils, keeping their skin moisturized.

2. Bathing: Dachshunds are generally clean dogs, but they may need a bath every three to four months, or as needed. Use a gentle dog shampoo and warm water to wash them. Be careful not to wet their long ears, as this may lead to infections. Thoroughly rinse off all shampoo residue to prevent skin irritation.

3. Nail Care: Dachshunds have small, delicate paws that require regular nail trimming. Long nails can cause discomfort and make it difficult for your Dachshund to walk properly. Use a quality dog nail clipper to trim the nails, being careful not to cut too close to the quick. If you are unsure, consult your veterinarian or a professional groomer for guidance.

4. Dental Hygiene: Like all dogs, Dachshunds are prone to dental issues, such as plaque and tartar buildup, which can lead to gum disease and tooth loss. To maintain good dental hygiene, brush your Dachshund's teeth regularly using a dog-specific toothbrush and toothpaste. Additionally, provide dental chews or toys to help remove plaque and keep their teeth strong.

5. Ear Care: Dachshunds' long, floppy ears can trap moisture and debris, making them prone to infections. Regularly check their ears for redness, swelling, or a foul odor. Clean their ears using a vet-approved ear cleaner and cotton balls, gently wiping away any dirt or wax. Avoid inserting anything into the ear canal, as it can cause damage.

Remember, grooming is not just about maintaining your Dachshund's appearance; it's also an opportunity to bond with your pet. Make grooming sessions enjoyable by providing treats, praise, and a calm environment. If you feel overwhelmed or are unsure about any aspect of grooming, consult with a professional groomer or your veterinarian for further guidance.

By following these grooming tips, you can keep your Dachshund looking adorable, healthy, and happy, enhancing the bond between you and your furry companion.

Regular Veterinary Care and Preventive Measures

As a responsible pet owner, providing regular veterinary care and taking preventive measures are crucial in ensuring the health and well-being of your Dachshund. This subchapter will guide you through the essential steps you need to take to keep your furry friend in top shape.

Regular veterinary check-ups are essential for maintaining your Dachshund's overall health. Just like humans, dogs require routine visits to the veterinarian to prevent and detect any potential health issues. During these check-ups, your veterinarian will perform a thorough examination, update vaccinations, and conduct necessary tests to ensure your Dachshund's optimum health.

Vaccinations are crucial in preventing various diseases that can be harmful to your Dachshund. Your veterinarian will recommend a vaccination schedule tailored specifically to your dog's needs. Core vaccines, such as rabies, distemper, parvovirus, and adenovirus, are essential for every Dachshund. Additionally, depending on your geographical location and lifestyle, your veterinarian may recommend other vaccines, such as leptospirosis or Bordetella.

Preventive measures, such as flea and tick control, heartworm prevention, and dental care, are vital in keeping your Dachshund healthy and happy. Fleas and ticks can cause discomfort and transmit diseases, so it's important to use effective flea and tick prevention products recommended by your veterinarian. Heartworm disease, which is transmitted through mosquito bites, can be fatal if left untreated. Administering monthly heartworm preventatives as prescribed by your veterinarian is crucial in protecting your Dachshund.

Dental hygiene is often overlooked but plays a significant role in your Dachshund's overall health. Regular brushing with dog-friendly toothpaste and providing dental chews can help prevent dental disease, which can lead to pain, infections, and other health complications. Your veterinarian may also recommend professional dental cleanings to ensure your Dachshund's teeth and gums are in optimal condition.

In addition to regular veterinary care, maintaining a healthy diet and exercise routine are essential for your Dachshund's well-being. A balanced diet tailored to their specific nutritional needs, along with regular exercise, will help maintain a healthy weight, prevent obesity-related health issues, and keep your Dachshund mentally and physically stimulated.

By following these guidelines for regular veterinary care and preventive measures, you'll be taking proactive steps to ensure your Dachshund has a long, happy, and healthy life. Remember, your veterinarian is your partner in your pet's care, so don't hesitate to reach out to them with any concerns or questions you may have along the way.

CONCLUSION

In conclusion, "Dachshund Survival Guide: How to Train Your Dachshund" has provided you with a detailed roadmap to understanding and training your Dachshund. From the foundational principles of patience and consistency to specific strategies tailored to this unique breed, this guide is designed to equip you with the knowledge and tools necessary for a successful training journey.

We've covered essential aspects of Dachshund care, including obedience training, socialization, and addressing specific behavioral issues, with a focus on practical, step-by-step methods. You now have strategies to effectively communicate with your Dachshund, harness their intelligence and eagerness to please, and build a lasting bond based on trust and mutual respect.

By applying the detailed advice and techniques provided in this guide, you can ensure that your Dachshund not only becomes well-trained but also enjoys a happy, healthy, and fulfilling life. Remember, training is an ongoing process that strengthens the bond between you and your Dachshund, and each day brings new opportunities for growth and learning.

Thank you for choosing this guide as your companion in the rewarding journey of raising a Dachshund. May the bond with your furry friend continue to grow stronger as you both navigate the exciting path ahead.

Made in the USA
Monee, IL
14 November 2024

70146554R00046